THE ALIEN JOKE BOOK

★★★★★★★★★★★★★★★★★★★★★★★★★★★★★★★★★★★★★★

★★★★★★★★★★★★★★★★★★★★★★★★★★★★★★★★★★★★★★

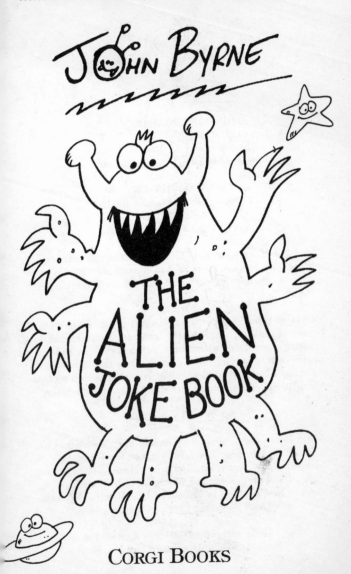

JOHN BYRNE

THE ALIEN JOKE BOOK

CORGI BOOKS

★★★★★★★★★★★★★★★★★★★★★★★★★★★★★★★★★★

THE ALIEN JOKE BOOK
A CORGI BOOK : 0 552 545627

First publication in Great Britain

PRINTING HISTORY
Corgi edition published 1997

Set in 12/15 pt Tiffany

Corgi Books are published by Transworld Publishers Ltd,
61-63 Uxbridge Road, Ealing, London W5 5SA,
in Australia by Transworld Publishers (Australia) Pty. Ltd,
15-25 Helles Avenue, Moorebank, NSW 2170,
and in New Zealand by Transworld Publishers (NZ) Ltd,
3 William Pickering Drive, Albany, Auckland.

Made and printed in Great Britain by
Mackays of Chatham PLC, Chatham, Kent

★★★★★★★★★★★★★★★★★★★★★★★★★★★★★★★★★★

★★★★★★★★★★★★★★★★★★★★★★★★★★★★★★★★★★★

FOREWORD

Greetings, r-readers, it's me again –
Quentin Quiver. And I'm b-boldly
going where nobody has g-gone before.

Well, maybe not boldly going.

I'm a little bit nervous about
f-floating around out here, but at least
I've found a way to escape all the
hustle and bustle of Planet Earth.

Things are just getting scarier and
scarier down there – especially with all
those horrible science fiction movies
you lot like so much.

And as for the jokes you laugh at ...
YUKK!

I've often heard that somewhere in
space there are creatures who are
much more intelligent and civilized
than Earthlings are (except for me, of
course!). So I decided to do some
exploring and try to find them.

While I'm up here, I've got all the peace and quiet I need to work on my own new joke book: *Quentin Quiver's Book of Well-behaved Wit and Heart-warming Humour*.

I'm sure you can't wait to read it.

And the best bit is that I don't even need to use my own paper and pens. You see, I've found this handy blank joke book floating out here.

As you can see, it's got shiny metal covers and it looks brand new ... at least it does now that I've wiped the icky green slime off it.

Though I can't say I've ever seen this kind of metal on Earth.

And the icky green slime hasn't actually gone away either.

In f-fact there s-seems to be a lot more of it than I th-thought.

And one more thing – if there's no n-noise in outer space, what's all that laughing I can hear?

THE JOKE'S ON YOU, QUENTIN! WE ALIENS, ROBOTS AND SPACE MONSTERS ARE INVADING THIS BOOK!

ARRRGH!

IF QUENTIN THINKS EARTH IS BAD, JUST WAIT TILL HE SEES WHAT'S LURKING IN SPACE... DO YOU DARE EXPLORE THIS JOKE BOOK?

HERE COME SOME JOKES TO WIPE THE SMILE OFF YOUR SPACE...

Chapter One

WHY DID QUENTIN QUIVER CROSS THE GALAXY?

TO GET AWAY FROM
THE ALIEN CHICKEN!!

AIEEEE! THIS IS
NOT WHAT I MEANT
BY WANTING TO
EGGS-PLORE OUTER
SPACE!!

What would you call an alien who was born on Mars, lived on Venus and died on Saturn?
Dead.

Why did the alien put a mouse in his space rocket?
He wanted to make a little go a long way.

What did Planet Earth say to Planet Saturn?
'You must give me a ring sometime.'

Which is the moon monster's least favourite day?
Sunday.

What do you call a space kangaroo?
An Austr-alien.

Which side of a spaceship is the safest
to sit in?
The inside.

Why don't space scientists like
studying moonrocks?
Because that's a very hard subject.

What do you call empty spacesuits?
Astro-noughts.

What did the astronaut say to the
invisible space monster?
'I haven't seen very much of you lately.'

What game do space monsters play
when it rains?
Moon-opoly.

What did the Dalek say to the chicken?

Eggs-terminate!

What do space monsters have on their toast?

Mars-malade.

Where do space monks live?

In a moon-astry.

What do robot scouts sing?

'Tin can, gooley gooley gooley ... '

What did the space monster say when it saw a rocket landing?
'Oh good – tinned food!'

First Alien: I hear you visited the Paper Planet. What was it like?
Second Alien: Tear-able.

'Doctor, Doctor – I keep thinking I'm a Martian!'
'Don't be silly – you're not from Mars, you're from Venus, just like me!'

Why did the alien keep metal polish in her rocket?
She wanted to rise and shine.

How does a robot eat his food?
He bolts it down.

WHY DO ROBOTS NEED TO EAT LOTS?

BECAUSE THEY ALWAYS LOOK "TIN"!

Did you hear about the alien with fourteen arms?
She was handy to have around.

Jack and Jill went up a hill,
(The hill was on the moon).
An alien was in the well
So Jack and Jill went ... ZOOM!

I'M AN ALIEN WELL MONSTER!

ARRGH! WE'RE NOT FEELING "WELL" AT ALL!!

JACK   JILL

ZOOM!

Alien: Doctor, Doctor – I keep thinking I'm a moon!
Doctor: What's come over you?
Alien: Several cows and a cat with a fiddle.

What do you call an alien magician?
A flying sorcerer.

Why did the alien step on a chocolate bar?
He wanted to set foot on Mars.

What is the alien's favourite soft drink?
Lemon and slime.

What's the most musical planet in the solar system?
Nep-tune.

Why is it easy to fool a space monster?
Because he has 2,450 legs to pull.

Why did the alien paint his spaceship
bright red?
He wanted a tomato saucer.

Why did the alien want a tomato
saucer?
No other ship could ketchup with it.

What's green and slimy and tells
stories with happy endings?
A fairy t-alien.

THIS IS THE
FAIRYTALE OF THE
ALIEN PRINCE
AND
PRINCESS...

WE LIVED HORRIBLY
EVER AFTER!

What did Captain Kirk say when he
wanted a pet dog?
'Beam me up a Scottie!'

What's smelly, has pointed ears and
lives on the Starship Enterprise?
Mr Sock.

Why did the space monster have green spots all over her body?
Because if she had purple ones she'd look silly.

Who swings through outer space on a creeper?
Starzan.

What do you call someone who's crazy about aliens?
An Astro-nut.

Why did the alien army send their soldiers to Mars?
So they could spend the whole day Martian up and down.

What happened to the robot with a sore throat?
It had to have its tin-sels out.

DOCTOR - I'VE GOT ROBOT FLU!

ARE YOU TAKING COD LIVER OIL?

NO... MOTOR OIL!

How do aliens go fishing?
With a plan-net.

DO YOU CATCH MANY FISH WITH ALIEN FISHING RODS?

WITH THIS MANY ARMS, WHO NEEDS A FISHING ROD?

NO FISHING

What kind of fish do they try to catch?
Starfish.

What's the worst kind of bait to use for Starfish?
Earth worms.

What do you call a mummy in a rocket?
Tutankha-moon.

How do aliens play badminton?
With a space shuttle.

When are moon monsters most scary?
When there's an eek-clipse.

****

Why did the alien policeman always
say 'Hello, Hello, Hello'?
Because he had three heads.

How many aliens does it take to launch
a rocket?
5 ... 4 ... 3 ... 2 ... 1.

Why did the alien leave his wristwatch
in his rocket?
He wanted to make time fly.

I NEVER FORGET MY
WRISTWATCH... I JUST
FORGET WHICH ONE IS
CORRECT!!

DON'T BE
LATE FOR MORE
JOKES IN THE
NEXT
CHAPTER!

Chapter Two

HOW MANY ROBOTS DOES IT TAKE TO CHANGE A LIGHT BULB?

Do robots like to eat raisins?
No, but they're very fond of electric currants.

Which planet has the hungriest aliens?
Chew-piter.

YUM! MY FAVOURITE SPACE SNACK – A QUENTIN QUIVER SANDWICH!

EEK! THIS ISN'T WHAT I MEANT BY BEING "WELL BRED"!

What do you call a broken spaceship?
An Unidentified Flying Reject.

What should you sing to an alien who's just arrived on this planet?
'Happy Earth-day to You'.

What's E.T.'s favourite TV show?
'Phone Home and Away'.

Did you hear about the short-sighted alien?
She went for an eye, eye, eye, eye, eye test.

★★★★★★★★★★★★★★★★★★★★★★★★★★★★★★★★★★★★

Where do the smelliest aliens live?
Somewhere in the garlic-sy.

What spaceships do smelly aliens drive?
Phew.F.O.s.

FROGS, SNAILS AND PUPPY-DOGS' TAILS...

IS THAT WHAT BOY ALIENS ARE MADE OF?

NO – WHAT YOUR BREATH SMELLS OF! PHEW!!

What kind of stories do insects like to read?
Sci-ants Fiction.

An alien had fifteen hands – which one did he use to steer his spaceship?
He didn't – he used the wheel.

What's the moon monster's favourite shampoo?
Wash and glow.

'Doctor, Doctor – I keep thinking I'm an alien!'
'Don't worry – my bill will bring you right down to earth!'

SNIFF! IT'S TERRIBLE, DOCTOR – I'VE GOT COLDS IN ALL MY NOSES!

Eye Doctor: Can you read the bottom line of my chart?
Alien: Sure – it says XYLMPZXIPZ.
Eye Doctor: Gosh! How did you get that right so quickly?
Alien: What do you expect? It is the name of my next-door neighbour.

First Robot: Can you tell me if the bulb on top of my head is working?
Second Robot: Yes, no, yes, no, yes, no, yes, no ...

'Doctor, Doctor – I think I'm turning into a rocket!'
'How would you feel if I cured you?'
'I'd be over the moon!'

Why did the alien pupil bring an apple to school?
Because he wanted to be creature's pet.

HOLD STILL OR I'LL NEVER BE ABLE TO SHOOT THE APPLE OFF!

I'D "APPLE-Y" BE SOMEWHERE ELSE RIGHT NOW!

What flowers grow on the other side of the moon?
Sun flowers.

'Boo! I'm a space monster!'
'You certainly are – you've got a lot of space between your ears!'

What did one lump of space rock say to the other lump of space rock?
'Meteor at the corner?'

What's the last thing an alien does
before going to sleep?
He switches off the satel-lite.

What do you call an alien in a Father
Christmas suit?
A U.F.Hohoho.

What do you call an alien nursery
rhyme?
A uni-verse.

Why is it expensive to holiday among
the stars?
Because the prices are astronomical.

What is the alien's favourite part of the
newspaper?
The star signs.

First Alien: I do wish we aliens didn't
have these green spotty noses.
Second Alien: Huh! Aliens from my
planet don't even have noses.
First Alien: Then how do you smell?
Second Alien: A lot nicer than you do!

Why should you keep an eye on a sick
alien?
In case he takes Saturn for the worse.

Why was the alien playing football in
his flying saucer?
He was practising for the cup.

OUCH! I
NEVER GET
A KICK OUT
OF THIS
EARTH GAME,
"FOOTBALL"!

What do you call an elderly Martian?
A grey-lien.

'Doctor, Doctor – I come from a planet
way, way up in the sky.'
'So why have you come to see an Earth
doctor like me?'
'I'm scared of heights.'

Alien: Waiter – there's a fly in my soup.
Waiter: I'm very sorry, sir – I'll bring
you a new bowl immediately.
Alien: I should think so – when I order
fly soup, I expect to find a lot more
than just one in there!

Why did the alien's rocket factory close
down?
*He couldn't get his business off the
ground.*

****

First Martian: Want to go and see
Independence Day?
Second Martian: Isn't that the film
where Planet Earth is saved from an
invasion?
First Martian: That's right.
Second Martian: No thanks – I prefer
movies with happy endings.

Where would you go to see Venusian
cows?
A science fiction moo-vie.

Why did the alien have a frog in his
spaceship?
He only wanted to go for a short hop.

Why didn't the space monster need a
musical instrument?
She already had her own horns.

YOU'VE GOT THREE PERSONAL
STEREOS – YOU MUST REALLY LIKE
MUSIC..

IT'S NOT THAT –
IT'S JUST THAT
I'VE GOT THREE
PAIRS OF
EARS!

Why did the alien put a washing
machine in his spaceship?
He wanted to go for a spin.

Which part of the alien's foot was
shaped like a planet?
His Plu-toe.

Have you heard about the new alien
diet?
*You only eat Earthlings who are under
300 calories.*

Why was there an alien spaceship in
the bathroom?
*Because someone had left the landing
light on.*

Which is the world's largest sea?
The galax-sea.

What do you call two space experts
having a fight?
Science friction.

YOU'RE A HORRIBLE,
NASTY, UGLY
LOOKING
CREATURE!!

OH WELL—IF
YOU'RE GOING
TO SAY NICE
THINGS LIKE
THAT, THERE'S
NO NEED FOR
US TO FIGHT
ANYMORE!

What did the giant alien say to the
midget alien?
'Let's play squash.'

First Alien: I looked out of my rocket
window the other day and saw a
tortoise flying past.
Second Alien: What would a tortoise be
doing in outer space?
First Alien: About two miles per hour.

Why do 1,000-eyed aliens make good
teachers?
*They're used to controlling lots of
pupils.*

Why did the alien fill his spaceship
with jelly and custard?
He wanted to make it go a trifle faster.

Have you heard the joke about the
time machine?
*No – but someone's going to tell me
tomorrow.*

WHY HAVE YOU FILLED
YOUR FLYING SAUCER
WITH HERBS?

I WANTED TO
HAVE A THYME
MACHINE!

TIME FOR YOU
TO ENJOY EVEN
MORE GALACTIC
GIGGLES IN
CHAPTER
THREE!

Chapter Three

WHAT'S BLACK
AND WHITE AND
RED ALL OVER?

OUTER SPACE
WILL BE, IF YOU ROTTEN
ALIENS DON'T GIVE ME
BACK MY TROUSERS!!

BLUSH!

BLUSH!!

BLUSH!

Why did the alien buy bird seed?
He wanted to grow some birds.

What's grey, craggy and zooms around
the Mediterranean Sea?
The Rocket of Gibraltar.

What's white and fluffy and full of
aliens?
A Mars mallow.

What did the triangular alien say to
the square alien?
'I haven't seen you around for ages.'

Where would you catch the space
train?
At the space station.

Why didn't the six-armed alien need
petrol in her spaceship?
Because many hands make flight work.

Why was the alien crossing his legs?
He was dying to go to the Loo.F.O.

Why was the alien crossing his legs?
He was dying to go to the Loo.F.O.

Where do aliens go for their medicine?
Space Boots.

First Alien: On my planet, Pluto, it's far too cold to walk and you can't use flying saucers because the engines freeze up.
Second Alien: So how do you travel about the place?
First Alien: By icicle.

Why did the alien wear purple trousers?
They matched his purple hair.

THANK YOU FOR COMPLIMENTING ME ON MY NEW CLOTHES!

WHAT **I** ACTUALLY **SAID** WAS: "YOU LOOK LIKE NOTHING ON EARTH"!

Why did the alien climb into his spaceship's petrol tank?
He liked making a fuel of himself.

★★★★★★★★★★★★★★★★★★★★★★★★★★★★★★

What is the alien's favourite subject at
school?
Arts and spacecrafts.

What do you call an alien with three
eyes?
An aliiien.

What do aliens put on their Christmas
cake?
Star-zipan.

Why didn't the left-handed alien
appear in the space movie?
He wasn't right for the part.

What do you call a group of aliens in
their underpants?
Star Trek – the knicks generation.

Why did the alien fill his spaceship
with metal fasteners?
He wanted to give it a bit more zip.

Why did the alien have Planet Earth
painted on her glasses?
Because she wanted to see the world.

I'M REALLY PLEASED WITH MY NEW GLASSES!

NOW YOU CAN GO DOWN TO EARTH AND MAKE A SPECTACLE OF YOURSELF!

What's the quickest way to spot an
alien?
Give it chickenpox.

What is the astronaut's motto?
*'If at first you don't succeed, fly, fly
again.'*

Why did the kangaroo carry an alien in
his pouch?
Because he was a Mars-upial.

Why did the robot have a light on top
of his head?
Just in case he had any bright ideas.

What's the most boring science fiction
movie?
Snore Wars.

What's nasty, breathes heavily and
shouts 'One hundred and eighty'?
Darts Vader.

What's white, has a hole in the middle
and flies to the moon?
An Apollo mint.

Why do space monsters have bad
breath?
*It takes a long time to brush 1,578,246
teeth.*

Why don't space monsters know they have bad breath?
Would YOU tell someone who had 1,578,246 teeth?

When do aliens get their feet stuck together?
Once in a glue moon.

What do you say to a smelly alien on her birthday?
'For cheese a jolly good fellow.'

What did one moon monster say to the other moon monster?
'Here we glow, here we glow, here we glow!'

What do you call an alien with feet shaped like stars?
Twinkle toes.

How do moon monsters watch Earth TV?
Through their telly-scopes.

What's the spiciest planet in the solar system?
Mer-curry.

Why do donkeys know a lot about aliens?
Because they're good at ass-tronomy.

I SAY, I SAY, I SAY... HAVE YOU HEARD ABOUT THE ALIEN DONKEY?

YES—ITS FACE WAS HEE-HAW-RIBLE!

★★★★★★★★★★★★★★★★★★★★★★★★★★★★★★★★★★

Why should you never let aliens from
Saturn use your bath?
They might leave rings.

First Scientist: I thought I told you to
take that space creature to the
museum.
Second Scientist: I did – but now he
wants to go the cinema.

Why did the alien have two dogs in his
spaceship?
He wanted to go pup, pup and away.

What's the slowest thing in the galaxy?
A snail-ien.

★★★★★★★★★★★★★★★★★★★★★★★★★★★★★★★★★★★★

What did the robot say to the petrol pump?
'Take your finger out of your ear when I'm talking to you.'

STILL IGNORING ME, EARTH ROBOT? WELL, I'VE HAD MY FILL OF YOU!!

What do you call a clumsy space explorer?
A disastronaut.

Knock, knock!
Who's there?
Orbit.
Orbit who?
Orbit earlier on I got locked out of the spaceship.

What did the robot have for its tea?
Fish and computer chips.

What do you call a robot that eats lots of chips?
Heavy Metal.

What has six arms and two wheels?
An alien on a bicycle.

First Alien: Is this flying saucer running on time?
Second Alien: No, it's running on petrol.

What do you call a Martian on Saturn?
Lost.

What do you call an alien with 3,000 arms?
Andy.

I HEAR YOU'VE FALLEN FOR THE ALIEN WITH 3,000 ARMS AND HANDS...

YES-IT'S A REAL GLOVE STORY!

What do you call a rocket full of scientists?
A tube of smarties.

What's green and hairy and goes up and down?
A gooseberry in a rocket.

Why did the robot have a lid on top of his head?
Because he was always changing his mind.

Earthling: Do all aliens have super powered memories?
Alien: I forget.

Where do astronauts keep their sandwiches?
In their launch boxes.

Chapter Four

WHAT TIME IS IT
WHEN QUENTIN
SITS IN THE
SPACESHIP?

What do you get from an alien
butcher's shop?
Meat-eors.

DON'T YOU WANT TO SAMPLE AN ALIEN BURGER?

NO WAY— IT LOOKS LIKE IT COULD BE ME WHO ENDS UP BITING THE DUST!

What is an alien's favourite kind of
tea?
Gravi-tea.

What do you find locked up in space
prison?
Jail-iens.

THIS IS WHAT HAPPENS WHEN YOU TRY TO COMMIT A CRIME BUT YOU DON'T "PLANET" PROPERLY!

★★★★★★★★★★★★★★★★★★★★★★★★★★★★★★★★★★

What was the six-legged alien's favourite sport?
Foot-foot-foot-foot-foot-football.

Which TV channel do robots watch?
Beep.Beep.C.

Why was no-one scared of the six-legged alien monster?
Because he was armless.

Why are aliens good at art?
Because all their drawings are Mars-terpieces.

Why do alien barbers reach Earth before any of their friends?
Because they know all the short cuts.

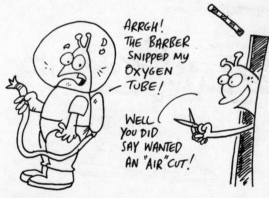

ARRGH! THE BARBER SNIPPED MY OXYGEN TUBE!

WELL YOU DID SAY WANTED AN "AIR" CUT!

What do moon monsters wear when
they go cycling?
Their bicycle eclipse.

What are green and slimy and keep
hitting themselves on the head with
hammers?
Nail-iens.

What do you get if you put an elephant
in a rocket?
A not-very-much-spaceship.

What's shiny and wears a kilt?
Robot the Bruce.

What kind of spaceship do space
detectives drive?
Snoopersonic ones.

THAT'S AMAZING,
SHERLOCK ALIEN –
YOU GUESSED THE
COLOUR OF THE
SUN WITHOUT EVEN
LOOKING!

YELLOW-MENTARY,
MY DEAR WATSON

****

Alien Customer: Hey! When am I going
to get served?
Alien Waiter: Hang on – I've only got
four pairs of hands!

What do you call an alien with a cold?
An Atishyoo.F.O.

Did you hear about the alien with two
bottoms?
He believed in chair and chair alike.

What did the Moon say to the Earth?
*'I'm not going around with you any
more.'*

Earthling: If this spaceship turns
upside down will we fall out?
Alien: No – I'll still speak to you.

What do you say to an alien with
sixteen sets of teeth?
'Fangs a lot.'

What do you call a dog in a spaceship?
An astromutt.

WHY WASN'T THE SPACE
DOG AFRAID OF THE ALIEN COMPUTER?

BECAUSE HIS BARK
WAS WORSE THAN MY
BYTE!

What do you say when an alien buys a
lottery ticket?
'It could be U.F.O.'

Why did the alien win all his golf
matches?
He kept scoring black holes in one.

How does an alien count to 100?
On her fingers.

What do you call a Gaul in a spacesuit?
An Asterix-naut.

****

Did you hear the joke about the time machine?
It goes in one year and out the other.

'Waiter – there's a spaceship in my soup!'
'Yes, sir, it's moon-estrone.'

What do aliens write on their holiday postcards?
'Wish U.F.O. were here.'

★★

What do you call a sick space monster?
A pale-ien.

What did the space explorers say when
they were captured by the vegetable
aliens?
'Peas release us!'

Why do aliens make good gardeners?
Because they've got green fingers.

Why is a meteor like a centre forward?
Because it's a shooting star.

AT OUR LAST ALIEN
FOOTBALL MATCH, THE
RESULT WAS 100 ALL!

WAS THAT
THE NUMBER
OF GOALS?

NO - THE NUMBER
OF LEGS ON EACH
PLAYER!

What time was it when the space
monster swallowed the Prime
Minister?
Ate P.M.

Science Teacher: Can you name ten different aliens you might find in outer space?
Pupil: Yes, sir – a Martian, a Venusian and eight aliens from Saturn.

Police Officer: I'm giving you a speeding ticket – you were doing at least 100 m.p.h. in that spaceship. Now, what's your name?
Alien: Xarblflymxsynxmzptlnyx.
Police Officer: On second thoughts, I think I'll let you off with a warning this time ...

Why did the robot stick a magnet on its nose?
It wanted to make itself more attractive.

WHY DID THE ALIEN PUT A BAG OVER HIS HEAD?

HE DIDN'T WANT PEOPLE LIKING HIM FOR HIS GOOD LOOKS ALONE!

Earthling: What's life inside a rocket like?
Alien: It has its ups and downs.

What books do bashful aliens like to read?
Shy-ence fiction.

Space Explorer: I've been flying my spaceship around the galaxy for over fifty years.
Alien: Really? You'd think you'd have reached where you were going by now.

First Robot: Fancy a game of tennis?
Second Robot: No thanks – I'm a little rusty.

WHY DON'T ALIENS LIKE TENNIS?

BECAUSE WE'RE BETTER AT BAD-MOON-TON!

Why did the alien fill his space station with chewing gum?
He wanted to perform some ex-spearmints.

OH NO! THE BUBBLE GUM'S LIFTED HIM OFF THE GROUND!

HE'S BECOME A "CHEW.F.O"!

Which alien was king of the wild frontier?
Davy Rocket.

What do you get if you cross a spaceship with a train?
A Choochoo.F.O.

How do skunks study astronomy?
Through their smellyscopes.

What do you get if you cross a robot with a chicken?
A battery hen.

First Alien: Is there intelligent life on
this planet?
Second Alien: No – I'm only visiting.

Why did the alien put feathers in his
spaceship?
He wanted to travel at light speed.

What do robots sing when they get
impatient?
'Wire we waiting?'

****

Chapter Five

KNOCK, KNOCK!
WHO'S THERE?
U.F.O.
U.F.O. WHO?

U WILL
F IND
O UT WHEN I CATCH YOU!!

'ORRIBLE ALIEN TENTACLE!

ARRRGH!

QUENTIN LEAVING PAGE AT LIGHT SPEED!

*************** 53 ***************

What did the alien say when the witch turned him into a frog?

Nothing – he's never looked better!

What did the aliens say when they played chess in their space station?
'The game's up.'

How do space explorers tie their shoelaces?
With astro-knots.

'Doctor, Doctor – I keep thinking I'm an alien.'
'Nonsense – you just need a holiday.'
'You're right – I've heard Mars is very nice at this time of year … '

Alien: Captain, would you shout at me for something I didn't do?
Captain: Of course not.
Alien: Good – I didn't put enough petrol in this spaceship.

Alien: How much is a return spaceflight?
Starship Captain: Where to?
Alien: Back here, of course.

What do you get if you cross a robot with a teddy bear?
Tinny the Pooh.

IS THERE MUCH FUR ON A ROBOT TEDDY?

BEAR-LY ANY AT ALL!

Doctor: Your face is green, your eyes are red and your tongue is grey!
Alien: Thank goodness – I was afraid there might be something wrong with me.

What do you call a very old spaceship?
A dino-saucer.

What do space giants say?
'Fee-fi-U.F.O.-fum!'

What's the robot's motto?
'Look before you bleep.'

Why didn't the alien have a pedigree dog?
He preferred moon-grels.

What do you call a fairy tale about a princess and a robot?
Beauty and the Bleep.

Why did the robot go to the undertaker's?
Because his batteries were dead.

Where does Grandpa Alien sit?
In his rocket chair.

WHAT'S GRANDPA ALIEN'S ROBOT MADE OUT OF?

ANY OLD IRON!

Alien Mum: Why did you put a two-foot-long space snake in your sister's bed?
Alien Son: Because I couldn't find a five-foot-long space snake.

First Alien: You know, if it wasn't for those purple spots all over, you'd look just like my sister.
Second Alien: But I don't have purple spots all over.
First Alien: I know, but my sister does.

'Mum, when we go in our spaceship can I put on the radio?'
'No – you'll have to wear a safety belt like everyone else.'

How do polite robots sit at the dinner table?
Bolt upright.

Why are fingerless aliens no good at sewing?
Because they're all thumbs.

Alien: Mmm! Thanks for offering me a sweet, Earthling.
Earthling: Yes – but I wish you'd waited till I'd let go of it before you swallowed it.

I WISH I HAD TWENTY FINGERS LIKE EARTHLINGS DO!

WRONG! WE'VE ONLY GOT TEN FINGERS EACH!

UH-OH! LOOKS LIKE SOMEONE HE ATE IS DISAGREEING WITH HIM!

Why do space explorers go bald?
They don't get much fresh hair.

What do you get if you cross an elephant with a spaceship?
Great big holes all over the landing site.

Earthling: Why are you aliens wearing those yellow spacesuits?
Alien: So we can hide in custard.
Earthling: But I've never seen aliens hiding in my custard.
Alien: See? It works!

****

First Alien: Where on Planet Earth did
your sister land her spaceship?
Second Alien: Alaska.
First Alien: Don't bother, I'll ask her
myself.

What do the seven dwarf aliens sing?
'U.F.O., U.F.O., it's off to work we go...'

First Alien: Where are you from?
Second Alien: Neptune.
First Alien: What part?
Second Alien: All of me.

First Alien: I'm bored. Let's race our
spaceships.
Second Alien: What's the point? The
spaceships can move much faster than
we can.

Earthling: Ugh! What a horrible looking creature!

Alien: I know you are, but I like you anyway.

MIRROR, MIRROR ON THE WALL — WHEN EARTHLINGS SEE MY FACE — THEY BAWL!

CRACK!!

Why do space explorers go bald?
They don't get much fresh hair.

'Doctor, Doctor – I keep thinking I'm one of the cat people from Planet Zzong!'
'How long has this been going on?'
'Since I thought I was one of the kitten people from Planet Zzong.'

What should you remember before you step into an alien spacecraft?
Not to get carried away.

What's the wettest planet in the solar system.
U-rain-us.

Have you heard the one about the alien
who polishes robots?
Yes – it's a story of rags to switches.

Humpty Dumpty sat on the wall
And suddenly fell from his place.
He landed on top of an alien blob,
Now he's bouncing around outer space.

First Martian: How long were you on
Earth?
Second Martian: Fourteen metres from
tentacle to tentacle, the same as I am
on Mars!

The Owl and the Pussycat flew into
  space
In a beautiful pea green ship.
When it landed again there was only
  the cat
(There was not enough food for the
  trip).

First Alien: I've heard that there's a
place on Earth where Friday comes
before Thursday.
Second Alien: Really, where's that
then?
First Alien: In the dictionary.

What's pink, lives in outer space and
eats rocks?
A pink rock-eating space monster.

What's pink, lives in outer space and eats sand?
A pink rock-eating space monster on a diet.

What do you get if you cross a space monster with a dog?
No more visits from the postman.

What's bright orange and looks like an alien?
A bright orange alien.

What's got four ears, eight legs and two bottoms?
A robot with spare parts.

I HEAR YOU'VE GOT YOURSELF LOTS OF SPARE PARTS...

WELL YOU KNOW WHAT THEY SAY?

YEAH- TWO HEADS ARE BETTER THAN ONE!

****

What's blue and looks like an alien?
*A bright orange alien on a very cold
day.*

What's big and slimy and has red and
yellow spots?
A yellow spotted alien with measles.

Why did the alien stick a spike on the
end of his spaceship?
*Because otherwise it would have been
pointless.*

Why aren't space calendars heavy?
Because they're full of light years.

LOOKS LIKE A GOOD DAY FOR A QUENTIN SANDWICH!

NO FEAR! I'M CANCELLING THIS DATE RIGHT NOW!

MORE JOKES TO MAKE YOUR DAY IN THE NEXT CHAPTER!

Chapter Six

WHAT DO YOU GET IF YOU CROSS AN ALIEN WITH A SPACE MONSTER?

SOMETHING THAT'S *TWICE* AS DETERMINED TO CATCH QUENTIN QUIVER!!

EEK! MY REASONS FOR LEAVING THIS BOOK ARE GETTING BIGGER ALL THE TIME!

What do you get when you cross an alien with an alien?
Two very cross aliens.

WHY SHOULDN'T YOU MAKE A ROBOT ANGRY..?

BECAUSE HE MIGHT BLOW HIS TOP!!

First Alien: I'm having problems with my new space computer.
Second Alien: The one with the super power memory?
First Alien: Yes – I keep forgetting to switch it on.

'Doctor, Doctor – I keep thinking I'm the steering wheel of a spaceship.'
'Get a grip on yourself.'

What do you get if you cross ten aliens with Humpty Dumpty?
Ten green bottoms hanging on a wall.

★★★★★★★★★★★★★★★★★★★★★★★★★★★★★★★★

Alien: Give it to me straight, Doc – will I be able to fly through space after my operation?
Doctor: Of course you will.
Alien: Great – I could never afford a spaceship before!

'Have you seen that new science fiction film, *Escape from the Prison Planet*?'
'No – it hasn't been released yet.'

HOW DO ALIENS GET TO SEE MOVIES?

THEY GO TO CINE-MARS!!

Alien: I'm looking for an alien with one eye called Xzcxxplz.
Earthling: I don't think I know him – but maybe if you told me what his other eye is called ...

First Alien: Can I interest you in buying this handy computer?
Second Alien: No thanks – I already know how many hands I've got.

Why did the robot put prune juice in
his battery pack?
He wanted to keep going all night.

The Queen of Hearts
Had baked a tart,
An alien came and swiped it:
'The taste,' he said, 'is really bad –
That's just how aliens like it.'

Why did the alien fill his spaceship
with spaghetti and watches?
Just to pasta time.

Why didn't the alien buy a new rocket
launcher?
Because it cost a bomb.

What do you get if you cross a chicken
with a space monster?
A fowl creature.

First Alien: Put away your rocket
launcher! This is a birthday party!
Second Alien: I know – but you told me
to blow up the balloons!

What do you call an alien with no ears?
Anything you like – she can't hear you.

I **SAID** "WHAT DO YOU CALL AN ALIEN WITH NO EARS?"

SORRY – CAN'T HEAR YOU...

Little Jill Horner
Sat in the corner –
A very courageous feat:
Her brother, Jack Horner,
Had forgotten to warn her
That this was the alien's seat.

Why couldn't the alien dance?
He had two left feet.

First Space Monster: What was that Earthling I saw you with last night called?
Second Space Monster: Dinner.

Space Monster: I'd like an Earthling sandwich, please.

Alien Waiter: I'm sorry, we couldn't possibly do that.

Space Monster: You mean you don't have any Earthlings?

Alien Waiter: Of course we do – but we're out of big slices of bread.

'Doctor, Doctor – I keep thinking I'm an alien.'

'How's your appetite?'

'Not good – I haven't eaten anybody in days.

I WONDER IF AN EARTH DOCTOR COULD HAVE ANY IDEAS ABOUT HOW TO CURE MY SPACE MONSTER TUMMY ACHE?

WELL YOU COULD START BY LETTING ME **OUT** OF HERE!

First Space Explorer: Did you see how I made those aliens run?

Second Space Explorer: Yes – they chased you all the way back to your spaceship.

★★★★★★★★★★★★★★★★★★★★★★★★★★★★

How do you stop an alien from smelling?
Tie a knot in its nose.

First Space Explorer: Why are you covering yourself with strawberry jam?
Second Space Explorer: To keep aliens away.
First Space Explorer: But there are no aliens on this planet.
Second Space Explorer: See how well it works?

PERHAPS IF I HIDE IN THIS SPACE JAM FOR LONG ENOUGH I'LL AVOID A STICKY END!

ASTRO JAM

Alien: I wish you Earthlings wouldn't play jokes on visitors.
Earthling: What do you mean? You asked me the time and I told it to you.
Alien: I know – but I asked someone else this morning and he gave me a completely different answer.

★★★★★★★★★★★★★★★★★★★★★★★★★★★★★★

Alien: Is this what you Earth people call a fish restaurant?
Waiter: That's right, sir – why do you ask?
Alien: Because I can't see any fish eating here.

Where would you find the biggest aliens in the galaxy?
If they are that big, they're hardly likely to get lost.

What did the hungry alien say to the Earthling?
'Take me to your larder.'

Why is the letter Y like an alien?
Because it's right at the end of the galaxy.

WE ALIENS LIKE TO LEARN THE ALPHABIT!

DON'T YOU MEAN "THE ALPHA-BET"?

NOT AFTER WE TAKE A BITE OUT OF IT!

What goes Mooz Mooz?
A spaceship flying backwards.

What goes Mooz Mooz Zoom Zoom
Crash?
*A spaceship flying forwards meeting a
spaceship flying backwards.*

Alien: This is a really horrible painting.
What kind of art do you Earthlings call
this?
Earthling: A mirror.

First Space Explorer: On my last
mission I caught three Martians, two
Neptunians and four Moonfers.
Second Space Explorer: What's a
Moonfer?
First Space Explorer: To light up the
night sky, stupid!

What do you get when you cross a
parrot with an alien?
Not very Pretty Polly.

What do you get when you cross an
alien with a steamroller?
A very flat alien.

What do you do when you see an alien?
Hope that the alien hasn't seen you.

What has legs like an alien, teeth like
an alien, tentacles like an alien and is
the same colour as an alien?
A picture of an alien.

First Alien: Do spaceships often crash
on this planet?
Second Alien: No – most of them only
do it once.

Where do aliens cook their breakfast?
In an unidentified frying object.

Earthling: I can play the piano by ear.
Alien: And you say we aliens are weird!
Why can't you use your hands like
everyone else?

How do you know you've landed on the
Planet of the Smelly Aliens?
You have a terrible stinking feeling.

Earthling: You aliens think you're
strong but I can lift an elephant with
one hand.
Alien: Go on, then.
Earthling: Sorry – first you've got to
find me an elephant with one hand.

Alien Teacher: A comet is a star with a
tail, but can anybody name a famous
one?
Alien Pupil: Lassie.

****

What do alien pupils play on the blackboard when teacher's not looking?
Astronauts and crosses.

Alien: Doctor, Doctor – I was fixing my robot and I swallowed the spanner.
Doctor: Are you choking?
Alien: No, I'm serious.

Newsreader: I've got good news and bad news. The good news is that scientists have announced that there aren't any big frightening aliens in outer space.
  The bad news is that they've all landed down here.

Why didn't the science fiction film have any stars?
A space monster ate them all.

Chapter Seven

'DOCTOR, DOCTOR — THERE ARE ROBOTS EVERYWHERE!'

'NONSENSE — YOU NEED TO HAVE YOUR HEAD EXAMINED.'

'CAN YOU DO THAT FOR ME, DOCTOR?'

SURE - BUT YOU'LL HAVE TO LET ME PULL YOUR HEAD OFF, FIRST!

CLICK! POP! WHIRR!

YEEK!! LET ME OUT OF THIS BOOK BEFORE I GO TO PIECES!!

Why do aliens fly around outer space?
Because it's too far to walk.

WHAT DO YOU SAY TO A FLYING ALIEN?

AIR WE GO, AIR WE GO, AIR WE GO!

A space monster ate one Earthling out of a group of ten. How many were left?
None – the others all ran away.

What are a space monster's three favourite foods?
Men, women and children.

An alien and an Earthling had an argument about which of them could jump higher than the moon. Who was right?
Both of them – the moon can't jump.

What did the alien bring back from his seaside holiday?
A stick of rocket.

Why are some aliens green?
So you can tell them apart from the blue ones.

How does James Bond travel through space?
In a spying saucer.

What do aliens have that no other creature in the universe has?
Baby aliens.

What do you call a space monster that writes lots of letters?
A mail-ien.

I WONDER IF QUENTIN WOULD MAKE A GOOD STAMP FOR MY LETTER?

I'M NOT STICKING AROUND TO FIND OUT!

Why does a rocket roar?
You would too, if your bottom was on fire.

What parts of Earth are in outer space?
The letters E, A, R and T.

Alien: Why do you humans have your nose in the middle of your face?
Earthling: Because it's the scenter.

THAT ALIEN MUST HAVE THE BIGGEST NOSE IN THE GALAXY!

"FOR SNEEZE A JOLLY GOOD FELLOW"

Knock, knock!
Who's there?
Wendy.
Wendy who?
Wendy countdown is over this rocket can take off.

Why did the robot drink a pint of grease before it went to bed?
It wanted to wake up oily in the morning.

What did the mummy alien do when she found the baby alien eating his joke book?
Took the words right out of his mouth.

'Do you like watching science fiction
movies on the television?'
*'Yes – but it's much more comfortable to
sit on the sofa.'*

How do aliens make their space boots
last?
They make their suits and helmets first.

What's green and slimy and has 4,000
legs?
100 forty-legged aliens.

Did you hear about the big hole that
has appeared on the surface of Mars?
Scientists are looking into it.

What does a mummy alien sing to her child?
'Rocket bye baby ... '

First Astronaut: There's an alien outside our ship with a really ugly face.
Second Astronaut: Tell him you've already got one.

Knock, knock!
Who's there?
Hugh.
Hugh who?
Hugh.F.O.

First Alien: I'm homesick.
Second Alien: But this planet is our home.
First Alien: I know ... and I'm sick of it.

Knock, knock!
Who's there?
Mandy.
Mandy who?
Mandy escape capsule – the rocket's
about to crash!

Alien: With only two legs, you
Earthlings can't be much good at
walking.
Earthling: I'll have you know I've been
walking since I was nine months old!
Alien: Really? You must be very tired.

What's the one thing an alien must do
before landing her spaceship?
Take off in her spaceship.

DON'T GET TOO CLOSE –
THE SPACESHIP'S
ABOUT TO TAKE
OFF!

I HOPE IT
DOESN'T
TAKE OFF
MUCH ...
I
BLUSH
VERY
EASILY!

First Earthling: Shall I offer the aliens
some of my homemade cake?
Second Earthling: Why? What have the
aliens ever done to us?

First Alien: I'm in a hurry to get to
Earth – will the next flying saucer be
long?
Second Alien: No, it will be round, the
same as usual.

LOOK! IT'S
A SQUARE
FLYING
SAUCER!

HE MUST
BE ON HIS
WAY TO THE
EDGE OF
THE GALAXY!

What is the robot's favourite city?
Electri-city.

What do you get from the space
monsters on the Ice planet?
Frost bite.

First Scientist: Do you need any special
training for moonrock collecting?
Second Scientist: No, you just pick it
up as you go along.

Did you hear about the spaceship that
landed in a convent?
It was a nun-identified flying object.

First Alien: All the Earthlings I've met have liked me on first sight.
Second Alien: Yes, it's usually on second sight that they go 'EEEEK!'

What do you call an alien's school homework?
An unidentified flying project.

What wears a spacesuit and carries a thermometer?
A nurse-tronaut.

Alien: Do people on this planet believe in free speech?
Earthling: Of course we do!
Alien: Good – can I use your telephone?

AREN'T YOU GOING TO PHONE E.T.?

I THOUGHT IT WOULD BE CHEAPER TO SEND HIM SOME LETTERS!

Earthling: Oh, look – this alien
restaurant serves 'Rocket Meals'.
Alien: That's right – they're very hard
to keep down.

What do you get if you cross a
spacesuit and a saddle?
A horse-tronaut.

The aliens conquered Venus, Jupiter
and then Mars, but when they reached
Earth they stopped. Why?
Because they ran out of conkers.

Alien: We aliens are much more
advanced than you. We've invented
radio.
Earthling: So what? We've got radio on
Earth too.
Alien: Yes – but ours is in colour.

Did you hear about the alien who flew
too near the sun?
He wanted to be the toast of the galaxy.

Alien: I bet my face is prettier than any
of your Earth flowers.
Earthling: Only if they're cauliflowers.

'There's a one-legged alien outside.'
'Tell him to hop it.'

Why did the astronaut throw a tube of
glue at the alien invaders?
*He wanted them to stick to their own
planet.*

Robot: My batteries are flat.
Alien: What shape are they supposed
to be?

Robot: My batteries are still flat. Can't you help me?
Alien: Yes – but I'm afraid I'm going to have to charge you.

Robot: The other robots are saying I'm mad!
Alien: Nonsense! You've just got a screw loose.

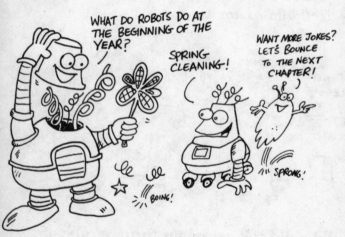

WHAT DO ROBOTS DO AT THE BEGINNING OF THE YEAR?

SPRING CLEANING!

BOING!

WANT MORE JOKES? LETS BOUNCE TO THE NEXT CHAPTER!

SPRONG!

Chapter Eight

WHAT'S THE DIFFERENCE BETWEEN A HORRIBLE SLIMY ALIEN AND A NASTY HAIRY ALIEN?

NOTHING! WE'RE BOTH OUT TO GET QUENTIN!!

OH NO! LOOKS LIKE I'M GOING TO GET SQUEEZED OUT OF THE BOOK FOR GOOD!

★★★★★★★★★★★★★★★★★★★★★★★★★★★★★★★★★

Why is an old spaceship like a baby?
It never goes anywhere without a rattle.

Earthling: I've heard that aliens can
read minds, but I don't believe it.
Alien: I knew you'd say that!

Mary, Mary, Quite Contrary,
Why doesn't your garden grow?
'It was still standing
Till an alien landing
Squashed it flat with his U.F.O.!'

'My father had a chat with an alien the
other day.'
'But aliens live in outer space!'
'I know – he really had to shout.'

Baby Space Monster: 'Mummy, I don't like Earthlings.'
Mummy Space Monster: 'Well, just leave them on the side of your plate.'

What do you call a cowardly spaceship?
An unidentified fleeing object.

I'M A SCAREDY-CAT SPACESHIP!

YES- AT THE FIRST SIGHT OF AN ALIEN HE TAKES FLIGHT!

First Space Monster: Why are you crying?
Second Space Monster: The Earthling I was chasing jumped into his rocket ship and flew away?
First Space Monster: Cheer up – you'll be able to find other Earthlings to eat.
Second Space Monster: No I won't – this one still has my false teeth stuck in him!

Why did the alien buy a pair of waterwings?
He was going into deep space.

Alien: I can't seem to get the hang of your Earth music at all.
Earthling: Haven't you been practising with the guitar I lent you?
Alien: I can't get a sound out of it, and I've been blowing it all night!

What do you get if you cross Darth Vader with a toad?
Star Warts.

First Space Explorer: We've been trapped on this desert planet for days now. This map is useless!
Second Space Explorer: You fool! That's not a map – it's a sheet of sandpaper!

WE'RE LOST–
I HOPE YOU'RE
NOT HOLDING
THAT EARTH
MAP
UPSIDE
DOWN...

...OS
THINK
I DON'T

Why did the huge space monster bite a chunk out of the sun?
He fancied a light snack.

First Alien: When I was flying back here, lots of Earthlings came to see me off.
Second Alien: I heard about that – they just wanted to make sure you were going.

Alien: I've got 3,000 bones in my body.
Earthling: That's amazing!
Alien: Not really – I had a can of sardines for lunch.

★★★★★★★★★★★★★★★★★★★★★★★★★★★★★★★

Earthling: Tell the truth – do you aliens think Earth people are pretty or ugly?
Alien: Both – you're all pretty ugly.

ONE THING I LIKE ABOUT HAVING ALL THESE HANDS – IT MAKES IT MUCH EASIER TO JUGGLE!

First Alien: Our visits are very good for Earthlings.
Second Alien: That's true – every time they see us, they go for a long healthy run.

How can you tell if an alien is rich?
He has a chauffeur-driven flying saucer.

★★

Astronaut: Help! My spaceship's
crashed into the sea and I can't swim!
Mission Controller: So what? I can't
play the guitar but I'm not shouting
about it!

First Alien: Just think – we've been on
Earth for a full twenty-four hours now.
Second Alien: Yes – and it seems like
only yesterday.

'Doctor, Doctor – every time I fly my
spaceship, my ears go pop!'
'That's easy to fix – try these boiled
sweets. There – is that any better?'
'Pardon? I can't hear with these
sweets in my ears.'

First Alien: Lots of Earthlings like this chocolate stuff, but I think it tastes disgusting.
Second Alien: Yes, but I think you're supposed to take it out of the wrapper first.

Earthling: We come in peace – give me your hand.
Alien: Why? Haven't you got one of your own?

'Mummy, Mummy – the other robots say I'm not a real electric robot. They say I'm only clockwork!'
'Nonsense, dear – they're just trying to wind you up.'

Why did the alien yank the tablecloth away?
She wanted to see some flying saucers.

Did you hear about the alien who tried to blow up an enemy spaceship?
He burnt his mouth on the exhaust pipe.

Can robots stand on their heads?
Yes – but they have to take them off first.

Why couldn't the alien play at Wimbledon?
He didn't have his tennis rocket.

★★★★★★★★★★★★★★★★★★★★★★★★★★★★★★★★★★★★★

Did you hear about the clumsy alien?
He broke the sound barrier.

What paper do aliens read?
News Out of the World.

Why didn't the alien realize he'd
landed in quicksand?
It took a long time to sink in.

Why did the astronaut put his pay
packet in a rocket?
He wanted to raise his salary.

Alien: We aliens have invented a
machine to make it rain.
Earthling: We Earthlings don't need a
machine – we just go out without an
umbrella.

What do you get if you cross *Free Willy*
with *E.T.*?
A whale-ien.

★★★★★★★★★★★★★★★★★★★★★★★★★★★★★

How does the moon monster keep his
toenails neat?
Eclipse them.

What's the smelliest part of a
spaceship?
The com-phew-ter.

How do you tell if a moon monster is
happy?
See if it's beaming.

WHEN'S THE BEST TIME TO READ AN ALIEN JOKE BOOK?

BY THE LIGHT OF A FOOL MOON!

Alien: You may be an Earthling but
you've got outer space teeth.
Earthling: What do you mean, 'outer
space teeth'?
Alien: Lots of big black holes.

First Space Explorer: What steps
should we take if we see an alien?
Second Space Explorer: Long ones in
the opposite direction.

Why don't aliens think much of
Earthlings?
Because they look down on us.

Alien Pupil: Sorry I'm late for school –
I was having a dream that I was flying
to Earth.
Alien Teacher: How can a dream make
you late for school?
Alien Pupil: I had to stop on Venus to
ask directions.

What's the difference between a rocket
and a fly?
Rockets can fly but flies can't rocket.

Alien Teacher: If I had two apples in
one hand and three apples in my other
hand, what would I have then?
Alien Pupil: You'd still have six more
hands with nothing in them!

Knock, knock!
Who's there?
Jupiter.
Jupiter who?
Jupiter lock on the spaceship after I
told you not to?

Space Explorer: Doctor, I've been
bitten by an alien!
Doctor: Don't worry – I'll put some
cream on it.
Space Explorer: Don't be silly – it'll be
back on its own planet by now!

What did the alien from Saturn think
of *The Alien Joke Book*?
*She Saturn her favourite chair and read
it from cover to cover.*

WOW! THAT ROCKET IS REALLY ENJOYING THE ALIEN JOKE BOOK!

WELL, HE WHO LAUGHS BLAST, LAUGHS LONGEST!

What did the alien from Mars think of
The Alien Joke Book?
He thought it was choc-full of laughter.

What did the Earthling think of *The
Alien Joke Book?*
You tell us!

AND
FINALLY ...

WE GIVE UP, QUENTIN— ONE MORE JOKE AND WE PROMISE YOU'LL NEVER BE TROUBLED BY THE ALIEN JOKE BOOK AGAIN!
JUST ONE MORE? IT'S A DEAL!!

WHY DID QUENTIN QUIVER CROSS THE GALAXY IN THE OTHER DIRECTION?